My Life in the
Saddle

WORKING WITH PONIES AND KIDS

Paul Down

Thanks to Ken, Sue and Malcolm
for all their help in producing this book.

Foreword

My life has been made up of two parts and most people who know me only know one part of me. On the one hand, I am a horse and pony lover who has spent most of his life riding, helping and teaching other pony-loving children, mainly through the UK Pony Club (the Pony Club is an international voluntary youth organisation for young people interested in ponies and riding), Riding for the Disabled (RDA), and The Duke of Edinburgh's Award scheme. On the other hand, others only know me as a Christian youth worker, working both in church and local authority youth work.

I am hoping that this story will bring the two together and help my children, grandchildren, and great-grandchildren understand something of their inheritance. Hopefully others too will learn why I am what I am and the input that God has had upon my life.

As I get older (I'm 91 years old at the time of writing this), my memory and sight are not what they once were. I have been diagnosed with mild cognitive impairment and severe arthritis in my spine and hips, so I apologise for any discrepancies in dates or detail. Most of the horse and pony part has been written for some time, but the writing of my life history and God's input into my life is fresh. I hope you will find in it a help and perhaps identify God's involvement in your life, even if it is unrecognised as yet. God is love and His love is being demonstrated if you care for others in any shape or form; you are doing God's work.

God bless you!

Contents

1

The Early Years
and Learning to Ride

I was born on 17th May 1929, the third son of Reginald and Nora Down at Wallington, Surrey. I remember Dad, a freelance commercial traveller, being away all week, returning on Friday afternoon. Saturday morning was spent sorting his sample cases. Dad was also a Pentecostal pastor with a small Assemblies of God church in Hackbridge, Surrey. Sunday was spent at church in the morning, at Sunday school in the afternoon, with an open-air meeting and other services in the evening. We finished the day singing hymns around the organ at home. In 1933 I started school at Bandon Hill Infants in Sandyland, Wallington, Surrey, now part of Greater London.

I am on the right of the picture with my four brothers, Mother and Grandmother.

I was always small for my age but in 1937 I had rheumatic fever and was expected to die. Rheumatic fever is a very rare complication that can develop after a bacterial throat infection. It can cause painful joints and health problems that affect the heart, joints and other organs. I remember the severe pain in my legs that meant I had to have a box cut out over my legs so that the bedclothes would not touch them. The loss of schooling left me retarded and feeling worthless. My parents were convinced that it was only their prayers, and those of their brothers and sisters, that got me through. I was off school for three months. I was sent down to Deal in Kent to stay with Mother's parents and two sisters to recuperate in the sea air.

With Grandad Windsor 1937 in Deal.

I remember my Auntie Con (Mum's twin) returning from Canada, and Uncle Percy (Mum's brother) and Auntie Edna with their children, Peter and Jane, returning on furlough from Malaya where he was supervisor of the Kuala Lumpur Rubber Estates.

My first mount 1938.

My memory then remains blank until the beginning of the war. Back in Wallington, an Anderson shelter was built in the garden in which sometimes slept Mum, Dad, us four boys, new baby brother Barrie, Nan (a midwife who stayed on as part of the family) and two elderly neighbours. Still being very small and not fully recovered, I was sent to Ashstead, Surrey, where my mum's parents and sisters had moved to from Deal. Deal, if I remember rightly, was totally evacuated as being unsafe from German attack. Auntie Glad lived in one house and looked after my two cousins, Peter and Jane. Their parents were back in Malaya looking after the rubber plantations and were later imprisoned by the Japanese army.

I was well looked after by my Auntie Glad, who took us to the local Anglican church each week. I remember nipping off to a Free church in the village at night, which was much more to my liking until Auntie Con, Mum's twin sister, arrived back from Canada and couldn't go back because of the war. I was ten years old when the war broke out in September 1939 and Dad, who was a freelance commercial traveller, lost all his income over night. This was mainly because clothing coupons were issued as clothing factories were put onto war work and there was no clothing to sell. A friend of his set up a warehouse in Loughborough for the few gents' socks and offered Dad the job managing it. On 19th November 1940, the night of the big German bomber raid on Coventry, we moved to Loughborough.

Loughborough

My two older brothers had attended grammar schools, so had no problem in being accepted into Loughborough College school. Dad persuaded them to take me despite having no 11-plus exam and being so far behind educationally. The school put me on to a copy book, where I had to literally copy the words written down to teach me to write properly, but I didn't understand most of the lessons, except Gym, which I loved and was good at.

Our home in Loughborough was an empty shop fairly close to local farmland and behind the house was a large field in which was an old horse and a pony. They belonged to a man by the name of Archie Moss who, before the war, had run a large livery stables and had then transferred to running taxis. There was an old (so I thought) man, an ex-Cavalry man, called Danny Roberts who looked after the animals and I soon got to know him and eventually he taught me to ride. He became a family friend and used to come and play chess with my father. Danny was a travelling barber and visited a large farm in Shepshed owned by one Freddy Mee. He had a number of ponies for his various child relations and Danny obtained permission for me to ride there, so I soon got experience of riding a number of different ponies. I wasn't keen on sports at school and, being small, never got picked for teams in any case so nearly always bunked off on games afternoons and went riding. I often went out and found the Quorn Hunt in the afternoons in Charnwood Forest, and soon became well enough known for people to ask me to ride their ponies for them. That sometimes meant cycling many miles to do so. The next few years found me riding many different ponies, usually ones that other children could not ride for various reasons. If I was offered a ride, I said yes first and then asked what was wrong with it. That's the way you learn.

The war seemed many miles away and there was almost no traffic on the roads so both cycling and riding was much safer than it is today. Regular gymkhanas in Loughborough Park were another favourite. Fancy dress, sack races, musical sacks were my speciality, and it was there that I first saw Bob Spoor, a well-known horse dealer who lived in the village of Quorn and for whom I later came to work.

During the holidays I worked on a local farm, in fact I came to spend every spare minute I had at the farm. It was there that I progressed onto horses. First the milk float horse – I only remember that it was uncomfortable! – and then on to Bill, the son's hunter, a blood horse who he asked me to ride one day to round up the cows which were several fields away from the farm. At the farthest point from the farm, in a very large field, the animal decided that it wanted to go home – and it did. It ran away with me and I was far too inexperienced to stop it. Round this huge field, flat out, I managed to steer it into a haystack where it dumped me and set off for home, scaring everyone when it galloped into the yard without me. I was none the worse for my fall but went back to ponies for some time!

2

The Livery Yard
and Show Jumping

In 1942 I was off school again with acute rheumatism, which kept me at home for a considerable period and I knew I had no hope of passing exams. When better, I spent all my spare time riding wherever I could find a pony to ride, skipping games lessons at school to do so. I spent every spare moment either riding or on Moss's farm, determined to prove that I was as fit as everyone else. One activity that got me fit was running alongside Moss's horse from pub to pub so that when he went inside, he had someone with him to hold on to the horse outside the pub! I was so fit, it seems, that I won the school's compulsory cross-country race on my last day at school, despite not being all that keen on cross-country running and having avoided doing it at school in favour of being with horses.

In 1945, with the end of the war in sight, my family returned from Loughborough to Wallington. I left school with no qualifications and no sense of worth. Mother tried to persuade me that my ability to ride and school ponies for other people was just as important as those skills of photography and printing that my brothers had, but it didn't help and I lived with this sense of unworthiness until the day I retired.

Our family at the end of the war.

I said I wanted to work with horses, so Dad contacted Bob Spoor's livery stables in Quorn. Bob agreed to take me on and pay me the princely sum of one pound a week plus board and lodging. There I got my first real experience of horses.

Hunters were what Bob specialised in. Several liveries had to be mucked out, groomed to perfection, and exercised every day. Sometimes I would ride one and lead one or two for an hour's road work and I was often in the saddle for several hours a day.

Me riding Silver at Bob Spoor's.

On other days I would fall in behind the hounds as they came through the village, riding one and leading one to ride second horse to Mrs Everard, who kept her horses with us and would drive to the meets in her pony and trap (no cars). She of course rode side-saddle and her favourite horse, when he came up from grass, was more like a Shire than a lady's horse but when he was clipped out, he could go cross country with the best. We also kept horses for a man called Sheldrake, mostly show jumpers, and I remember having to treat the famous show jumper, Umbo, who came to us with a fistulous whither. This is a painful, and potentially fatal, condition caused by the rubbing and irritation of poorly fitted equipment against a horse's sensitive shoulder. I had to treat the horse with hot poultices twice a day as in those days there were no antibiotics or modern treatments available. Before he went back, Bob gave me a jumping lesson on him, the only time I have ever jumped a six-foot fence! Sheldrake also had a racehorse which I had to take to Leicester races – it came last! That was my only visit to a race meeting.

Tony, 1946, at Bob Spoor's.

Bob purchased most of his horses for sale from Ireland and several times I remember going in the blackout to the local railway station late at night to unload horses that had arrived from Ireland. Bob would lead the way in the car with its restricted lights and I would ride one and lead two back to the stables. I think they were too seasick after their journey to give any trouble.

I returned home at the end of 1946 to work with Dad in the family business and spent part of two seasons show jumping with a local butcher. The worst sort of butcher, wrapping poles with hedgehog skins to make them jump, and no idea of proper training for jumping. He was also a coward. One Bank Holiday, when we were riding on Bookham Common, his big mare was "corned up". That means that in those days, to get a horse fit, you fed him on oats and the finest hay you could get like clover or lucerne. There was no such thing as pony nuts or the many proprietary feeds available today. The mare was playing up all the time and eventually he made me get on it and he rode his wife's little half-bred hackney that I had previously jumped. I was about seven-and-a-half stone and the mare promptly ran away with me around a crowded common. That was the second time that I was runaway with, both times as the result of older people who should have known better than to have put an inexperienced boy on a corned-up horse.

Ain't You Sorry, ridden by me, Chesham 1947.

3

The Army

May 17th, 1947. My eighteenth birthday and, having been called up for compulsory National Service, I was soon on the way to Cowley Barracks to do my basic training with the Oxford and Bucks Light Infantry, then on to Barford Camp at Barnard Castle where I was supposed to be trained as a wireless operator in armoured cars with the 12th Royal Lancers. I was just about to step onto an armoured car for the first time when an orderly arrived to say that the Colonel wanted to see me. Somehow, he had heard that I was interested in horses and asked me if I would like to become his groom! Needless to say, I jumped at the chance. In any case, you don't say no to your commanding officer! (The 12th Lancers were a famous Cavalry regiment and most of their senior officers were old Cavalry men, the younger ones all seemed to be the sons of famous Cavalry officers or the *Honourable This* or *That*!)

12th Royal Lancers, preparing to go on exercise at Barnard Castle Barracks.

Me with the Colonel's horse.

Colonel Burn's horse was a massive 17 hands, more like a Shire but looked OK when clipped out, and we soon had several horses in stables just off the official campsite. This expanded until we had twenty-one horses on and around the camp. The 11th Hussars were camped across the valley and also had horses so there was a great rivalry as to turn out of both horses and men. I had several men under me by then and was two tapes up (Corporal). (Tapes are the chevrons, worn on the arm, denoting the ranks of Lance Corporal, Corporal or Sergeant. In the picture of me with the Colonel's horse I have one tape, denoting Lance Corporal.) We were all dressed in World War One Cavalry dress i.e. jackets, breeches, puttees, boots and spurs, and were not allowed to ride off camp unless we were fully dressed. The officers hunted with the Zetland Hunt but, unfortunately, we never got the chance.

We did have two ex-regimental polo ponies in camp, both old, and I was the only one allowed to ride one, an old type 13.3 hands. I used to annoy the Regimental Sergeant Major, who was also an old Cavalry man, by riding this pony up the side of the parade ground bareback with just a halter on, changing legs every two strides.

One day, the Adjutant (the officer who helps the Commanding Officer with unit administration), one of the few officers who did not have his own horse, arranged for me to ride one of the ponies with him to a local gymkhana and for me to enter the show-jumping class.

It was some distance to hack but we did it, and duly jumped a reasonable round, but no rosettes. When we got back, the Adjutant was in serious trouble with the Colonel as the pony was supposed to be in retirement and he had not asked permission.

On another day, I was getting a meal in the canteen when I found myself standing beside Peter Robeson OBE, later of Olympic fame. He had just arrived in camp having refused to go for officer training. I soon arranged for him to join my team and he took over from me when I was demobbed. I had jumped against both Peter and his father in my short show-jumping career and spent a weekend at his home when he had leave to ride in a Point-to-Point race. He was, in my opinion, one of the finest classical riders there was and his eventual bronze medal wins in the 1956 (Stockholm, with his horse Scorchin) and 1964 (Tokyo, with his horse Firecrest) Olympic Games proved his ability.

It was in 1949, when I was due for demob, that I was faced with the fact that my life in the Army was anything but a Christian one. I was going home to a situation where everyone thought I was a Christian. I wanted to be one but didn't have the inner strength to stand out on my own. I was sleeping in a little room above the stables, away from the barracks, and I remember kneeling by my bed and saying to God, "I can't do this on my own. If you want me to follow you, you'll have to do something to help me."

He did.

Having been demobbed, I arrived home to find my brothers had all gone from the family home. I returned to work in the family clothing business. Our business, called Downland Garments, specialised in gents' trousers, but also midwives' uniforms and tropical suits, mainly for missionaries. We would buy the cloth from a Christian company in Bradford and have it made up to our specifications.

Knowing no-one, I booked to go to a Methodist guest house in Eastbourne. There I met the girl who was to become my wife. She had a voice like an angel and, before we left to go home – me to Croydon and her to Forest Hill – I was madly in love. Today, seventy-two years later, I still am!

With Jean on honeymoon, Shanklin, Isle of Wight.

Jean, my favourite picture.

Jean's quiet Christian faith has supported me through many tough times, without criticism. She has been my memory and my brains, although not sharing my love of horses and ponies and the time I have spent with them, she was, without doubt, God's answer to my prayers. For our first date, I cycled to Lewisham where Jean, a keen Lifebuoy (the junior reserve of the Boys' Brigade) leader, was refereeing a football match. She was also a member of the Lewisham Operatic Society and sang in local old folks' homes. Jean was also part of a group of young people from her church who, on a Sunday evening, would go to a lovely couple's home where they were loved and supported and I was welcomed into this group, feeling, for the first time, that I was part of a caring Christian group.

A lot of our courting was done at lunchtimes as Jean worked for the Bank of England in Finsbury Square. I worked nearby in Bow Lane when I wasn't out selling to the clothing shops.

Having got married in 1951, we soon moved from our one-roomed flat in Mum and Dad's South Croydon home, to a three-bedroomed house in West Croydon. We began worshipping at the West Croydon Methodist Mission where we became fully involved. I was not happy, however, with the lack of outreach to the local community so I became a helper at the local boys' club. I also became a founder member of the local Samaritans. Jean and I welcomed our three sons, Ken (1953), Andy (1959) and Malcolm (1961), into our new family whilst living in Croydon.

4

Youth Club Work

In 1958, I attended a one-month residential leadership training course where I shared a room with a chap called Roger Venables from Stafford, whose father was a founder of Holmcroft Youth Club in Stafford and wrote a booklet called *Christians in Youth Work*. Following this course, I more and more felt called to full-time youth work as I felt such an affinity with those, like myself, who felt worthless and uneducated. I discussed my feelings with my father, who very graciously released me from what was to then become the beginning of the end of his commercial clothing business, Downland Garments. As the previous leader had moved on, I was welcomed by the management committee and became the full-time boys' club leader of the Rectory Manor Boys' Club, one of two clubs belonging to the Croydon Boys' Club Trust. Sadly, 1960 saw the Boys' Club go up in flames on Guy Fawkes night and we were temporarily housed at our other club until we were able to move to another old school in Boston Road, Croydon.

These were tough boys in tough times. The coppers used to patrol in threes as the place where the Craig and Bentley murder took place is just round the corner from the club. On one occasion, when some boys and I were doing some alterations in the building, I mentioned that we needed some electrical cable. "That's no problem," one lad said.

"Well, where do we get it and how much will it cost?" I asked.

"Don't ask silly questions," came back the reply. "You want it, we will get it." And they did, I suspect off the back of a lorry!

We regularly went on all-night hikes. We would take the last train or bus out into some spot in the country and walk back overnight into Croydon, sometimes with strange results. On one occasion, walking back through downtown Croydon at about 4 o'clock in the morning, the lads kept chattering loudly and I had to keep reminding them to keep their voices down as people were asleep, when who should come round the corner but a bobby on night patrol. Seeing us, he wandered across the road, standing in front of us, looking right over my head, as these lads were all bigger than me. He says, "What do you think you're all doing at this time of the morning?" He then proceeded to give them a good verbal rousting and sent them on their way, totally ignoring me! I said nothing. The lads were not amused. I just said, "I told you to keep your voices down." There are some advantages to being small sometimes.

Following the Albemarle Report on a modern youth service, I was recognised by the government as a professional youth worker.

Life at the boys' club was often very demanding, so my Area Youth Officer had advised me to take up a hobby before I had a breakdown. I helped at Selsdon Park riding stables, clipping out horses for them, rode various horses for people, joined Warlingham riding club, and attended one of their riding courses. Here I achieved my first "**FIRST**".

I persuaded the riding club to sponsor six of my boys' club members to learn to ride on this course, paying for the hire of horses for them. It had not been done before and these were real City lads.

Rectory Manor Boys' Club boys under instruction at Warlingham.

I was in a class with a different instructor, one Nancy Peters IOH (Institute of the Horse, the forerunner to the British Horse Society). A real dragon with a heart of gold! Some months after the course I went to Reigate to see her at her own stables, saying, "I don't suppose you will remember me."

"Oh yes I do. You were the best of a bloody bad bunch," was her reply and agreed to take me on one day a week to train for my British Horse Society's Assistant Instructor (BHSAI) exam. Once a week on the old motorbike and sidecar, riding under instruction all morning with the other students, lunch in the flat with a theory session and jumping in the afternoon followed by sometimes taking a class. My first introduction to disabled riders was here as we sometimes had deaf and dumb riders and blind riders. During this time, I took a group of my club boys to Reigate on a Sunday. In the morning we fenced off a 40yd x 20yd area as a training area with post and rail fencing and, in the afternoon, I gave the boys a riding lesson.

In 1962, after failing the first time, I passed my BHSAI exam in the December and I was rather proud of the fact that it was the National Instructor for the British Horse Society who passed me. Brian Young was the first non-military National Instructor, and I had sat in on several courses he was taking. I also helped him in minor ways like moving jumps, etc.

5

First Over the Ridgeway

In 1963, I led a group made up of students and boys' club lads with the assistance of a doctor's wife who was training with me, to ride the recently opened Southdown's Ridgeway bridle route from Eastbourne to the Blue Boar Inn outside of Petersfield, where we duly all signed the book as "First Over the Ridgeway". We carried our own equipment in panniers that had been designed by the Pony Club and camped at pre-arranged sites on the way.

Croydon Boys' Club expedition instruction, 1963.

Boys' Club boys under my instruction at Nancy Peters' in the arena that they built.

Ron, Mrs Tucker, Mary, Betty and myself, on the first Ridgeway trek.

Mrs Tucker and Tommy on the Ridgeway.

Rest time for ponies on the South Downs.

Camping on the first trek, "Anyone for Supper".

Trekking past Chanctonbury Ring – prehistoric hill fort on the South Downs.

This had never been done before. Someone else had ridden the route stopping at night at B&Bs and stabling his horse, but we were the first to camp en route. This was my second "**FIRST**". We were met on the way by Mr Shippam of Shippam's meat pastes. He had been largely responsible for the opening of the Ridgeway route and had been a great help to us in fixing-up camping sites and had been a great encouragement to us.

6

A Pony Club
Visiting Instructor

In 1964, I was appointed as a Visiting Instructor for the Pony Club, then as a "B Test Examiner". This involved visiting Pony Club rallies and camps to instruct and test in "Riding and Stable Management". Two visits to the Anglesey Pony Club camp with Nancy Peters were great fun. We worked with real "hillbilly" kids who lived on local farms and hadn't got their own ponies. Some of the ponies they rode were kept on the sand dunes and couldn't cope with normal food because they ate the dune grass. If they were fed on good grass, they went down with "grass fever" as their stomachs could not cope with the rich food. Working with both the kids and ponies was very worthwhile. Also, a camp in the High Peak, with quite different kids, good ponies, and a jumping lane, is well remembered. A jumping lane is an enclosed lane with jumps in it where riders can practise jumping in safety. From then on, for the next twenty years or so, there were regular visits and camps for the South Down, North Staffs, and South Staffs Pony Clubs.

7

Henfield, Sussex and the Second Expedition

In 1965, having felt for some time the need to get back into mixed youth work, I was appointed as the first full-time leader at Henfield Youth Club in Sussex. In the short time at Henfield we achieved a lot.

I was soon involved in Pony Club activities with the local sub group of the South Downs branch. Several "Introduction to Riding" weekends with the Youth Service and then, in 1966, I organised, trained and led the first group of people (all teenagers) to ride the South Downs Ridgeway route both ways. This time we started from Mannings Farm, Small Dole, at the foot of the Downs. We rode through to Eastbourne and then back through to the extended end of the Ridgeway route near Petersfield in Hampshire. The mounts were all private ponies, so they had to get used to being turned out together, eating the same food and carrying panniers, tents, etc. Panniers were those approved by the Pony Club made from two Army valises joined with canvas by a saddler which fitted over the saddle. I also carried two tubular shoulder panniers and therein lies a story!

My horse went lame two weeks prior to us going and the whole project was in danger of being cancelled. Where could I find a fit horse, train it to carry panniers and get it used to the other horses, all in two weeks? A friend in Coulsdon had a Russian thoroughbred, 16.2 hands, very unpredictable with no manners, which sometimes became unrideable. I was told that if I were willing to take the risk it would do the mare good and I could borrow her. I did and had about ten days to prepare her. When we got the panniers on her, it took three people to get me onboard: one to hold her, one to give me a leg up and one to hold the stirrup on the offside. It was her or nothing; so, we risked it.

We duly set off and the first day's ride was like sitting on a bomb waiting to explode, but we survived. On the second morning, we climbed the big hill outside Lewes. As I went through the bridle gate at the top, she brushed the sides of the saddle bags on the gate posts. Down went her head between her front feet and she bucked and bucked until she had broken every strap holding panniers and equipment on her. I can't remember if I came off or not but I clearly remember all the others standing laughing at the rodeo. It took time to refasten everything with my spare well-oiled straps and leather bootlaces but strangely, from then on, she wasn't too bad and the hard work each day began to settle her down. Unfortunately, by the end of the week she began to go lame and on the last day I had to call for transport to take her home. The young people finished the ride on their own. A wonderful achievement which one of the girls reported on in the magazine *Riding* (no longer in existence). So ended my third "**FIRST**". We were greatly helped on this occasion by my local Area Youth Officer who was a brilliant cook and came each evening and prepared a hot meal for us all on two primus stoves.

The mare, they discovered later, had a hormone problem; every time she came in season, she went berserk. I believe she was put down eventually before she killed someone!

While we were in Henfield, I bought a strawberry roan Welsh mountain pony from Steyning market for the boys to learn to ride on. Shenandoah was a great character. He carried me over the Downs regularly and, when I broke him to harness, could stand up and wrap a pair of plough lines round himself like no other animal I have come across.

Taking a rest with my horse, Shenandoah.

It turned out that he had been in a riding school since he was two years old and had learnt all the tricks to get riders off. Ken, my eldest son, learnt to ride on him until we discovered that he had severe hay fever, from horses and other animals, which turned him off riding. I eventually sold the pony to a riding school owner for her own son to show jump as he was no novice ride.

It was while we were at Henfield that I was asked by Pony Club HQ to help write their book on mounted expeditions and also spent some time visiting various Pony Club branches lecturing on mounted expeditions.

In my days at Henfield there were two distinct parts. One, "the village" had its own hierarchy and was virtually run by the Women's Institute; and two, "the council estate" which did not get on with the village. The council estate had a few characters, one of which was the lad, whose name I forget, who, on my turning up at the club for my first evening, turned up at the same time. Finding that there was no official there to welcome me, and no sign of anyone with the key to let us both in, he just said, "Oh, that's no problem," and with a mighty kick he kicked the door in, breaking the lock!

There was also a boy named Sean. Sean had a reputation and one object in life, which was to show the village that he was "as good as any of them" and he had a horse to prove it! It seems that when he heard about this new club leader, he made it clear that he and it (that was me) were not going to get on. On hearing this, and that he had a horse, I sent him a message that I would like to see him. He duly turned up in all his cowboy clothes and I was able to tell him that I too liked horses and would love to see his. Eventually he dropped his aggression, and he did invite me to see his horse and his guns, and we got quite pally.

Although the horse and pony side of life was good during this period, the management of the Youth Service was not Christian and I was not happy with the lack of Christian opportunity, or so I thought in those days. I was therefore delighted to receive a phone call from my old roommate, Roger Venables, asking me whether I would consider moving to take up a position with the Holmcroft Youth Centre in Stafford, which I knew was a Christian club. We jumped at the opportunity and were there from 1967 for the next twenty-five years.

8

Stafford Days

Our time in Stafford was a period when, as Christians, we were re-learning how to witness to young people. Youth were changing, so we had to change our approach to them. No longer would young people be willing to sit in epilogues and be preached at. Our lives and how we lived and reacted to them counted more than what we said. This I fully believed but still struggled against the Pentecostal teaching of baptism in the Holy Spirit. Instead, I became a workaholic. "Saved to Serve" was the motto and, in my mind, I was a failure.

It was only at my retirement from work, when many people from the present, together with some old colleagues and senior officers who'd come out of retirement themselves and spoke highly of my work, that I realised that I was valued and didn't need to strive to be better. Over the years, with better teaching, I learnt that my work of caring for others was the work of the Holy Spirit in my life. God had used my own struggles and sicknesses to help other people.

We ran a number of different activities at the youth club, as well as those laid on by the authorities, such as art-and-craft competitions and inter-club sports days. Our canoeing group (the Gobi Desert Canoe Club), was well known, with many trips to the coast, local rivers and the River Wye. Our biggest problem in the club was drunkenness. We had a rule of no alcohol, so when members turned up drunk, we sat them down on the bank outside the building and plied them with strong coffee. We once found that our baseball bats had all gone missing and eventually discovered that they had been stolen by the boys to take up to Stoke-on-Trent on a Saturday night for pitched battles against the Stoke gangs.

It wasn't long before I became involved in taking young people pony trekking and running Horsemastership courses for young people from all over the Staffordshire area. For a couple of winters, we had a box load of trekking ponies boarded out with young people round Stafford for the winter, which was great for the youngsters, and saved the ponies from having to be sold and gave them a rest. I was also soon involved in helping both North and South Staffs Pony Club branches as a Visiting Instructor.

My fourth "**FIRST**" came about because my County Youth Officer contacted the Pony Club HQ to ask if they could recommend someone to train a young person to undertake a mounted expedition at Gold level for the Duke of Edinburgh's Award scheme. To her surprise she was given my name (one of her own staff!). I trained the girl, and the group working with her, and assessed her expedition in the Peak District. The first time a mounted expedition had been undertaken at Gold level which involved a three-day ride. I also had several other youngsters round the county who were doing Riding and Horsemastership for their DofE Award who I had to visit and assess.

Injury and Twenty Years of No Riding

I bought a 15.1 hand unregistered three-year-old thoroughbred that had failed to grow and had been turned out and virtually forgotten. She was very thin but this was my one chance to own a good blood horse. She was supposed to have been broken but was totally unschooled and a typical mad chestnut mare, so I re-broke her and rode out on to Cannock Chase every day. Unable to compete with her, I lent her to a Pony Club girl who promptly took her into the local Pony Club Eventing team and helped to win the Regional Cross Country competition. Unfortunately, she went lame and they returned her to me as they wanted a larger horse. She was soon sound again and very fit, but I had to sell her as I couldn't afford to keep her.

I was back to Pony trekking again and on one occasion pulled my shoulder muscle very badly on an ex-trotter. That put paid to my riding for about the next twenty years.

Retirement and Riding for the Disabled

After I retired, I got involved with the Riding for the Disabled Association (RDA) and eventually began instructing for the Stafford branch. A very satisfying time taking two classes each week of about five pupils on a Monday from two different "special needs" schools.

In 2004, at the age of 75 and with fairly severe arthritis in my lower spine, I started riding again with

RDA, and in October 2008 commenced with some others training for a dressage competition. Here, I had my first proper riding lessons since I trained for my BHSAI back in 1962 (46 years).

9

Getting Serious

In 2009, we celebrated my 80th birthday and, three days later, on May 20th, a group of nine from the Stafford branch of Riding for the Disabled went to Solihull Riding Club with voluntary helpers to take part in the RDA regional competition at beginner level. I rode my first ever dressage competition being the **FIRST** 80-year-old – the oldest person ever to do so, I have been informed. In the "Introduction to Dressage" test, in which we were all taking part, I came first with an 88.85 per cent score. In my second test, which was a qualifier for the National Championships, I also came first with a score of 75 per cent.

My first dressage Regional Competition.

Preparing to go into the dressage arena.

This gave me automatic entry to the National finals at Hartpury College in Gloucestershire which I attended with my retinue of helpers on July 12th. I took part in two competitions and came second in the "Freestyle" test, a nerve-racking experience for anyone but at my age, being at least fifty years older than any other competitor, quite satisfying.

My first National dressage test at 80 years old.

2010 was not a good year. Horses in the stables went down with a cough a few days before the competition and no horses were allowed off the site. In typical RDA fashion, someone from another branch lent us a cob to ride (the one I beat into second place the previous year and it beat me in the National) but I only had about fifteen minutes on it before the test and, not surprisingly, I came nowhere. In 2011, on a smaller animal, I hoped to do better.

In 2011, no longer a novice, I rode Rosie, a lovely looking and well-trained pony, but unfortunately quite scatty.

Rosie on my second time at the National dressage competition.

At the Regional competition, she saw the drop into the next field through the fence and was halfway through the test before she settled down. At the Nationals, again, she was frightened by a group of people popping up behind a fence and couldn't concentrate until she was halfway through the test. We didn't win!

Eventually, I had to give up teaching as my arthritis got so bad I couldn't stand for long enough to take a lesson. Fortunately, I could still ride as my pain was less severe when I was mounted than at any other time. It was a sad day for me when I had to give up teaching. To see a child who couldn't sit up straight on a pony slowly begin to sit up and take an interest in life, or to see a helper with no experience of horses or ponies but just a desire to help disabled children develop into an instructor themselves is very satisfying.

As I approach my 92nd birthday, the COVID-19 pandemic is beginning to come to an end and both the stables, and I, are still in lockdown. As riding helped my back immensely, I am now suffering considerable pain most of the time so I, along with other disabled riders, are praying for the day when we can ride again.

Appendix

Riding for boys' club

THE KEYSTONE COPS, a group of men under the chairmanship of the Earl of Westmorland, have established a fund from which to make grants to boys' club projects which would not normally be eligible for grant aid.

From this fund, a grant was made to Mr. Paul Down, a professional youth leader at the Rectory Manor Centre of the Croydon Boys' Club, to enable him to study for his British Horse Society Assistant Instructor's Certificate, under Miss Nancy Peters, I.O.H., of Reigate Heath Riding School.

As far as I know, Mr. Down is the only full-time youth leader with a B.H.S.A.I. certificate and who is also a Visiting Instructor for the Pony Club.

The Croydon Boys' Club has a riding section and has been awarded bursaries by the Warlingham and District Horse Club which have allowed eight boys to attend riding instruction classes and to take their National Riding Clubs Grade I certificate.

These boys are a great help at horse shows and horse trials in the Warlingham area as jump stewards. Mr. Down is seeking to introduce riding and pony trekking as an activity in boys' clubs in Middlesex and Surrey.

Horse & Hound, March 2nd 1963

FIRST RIDERS OVER NEW BRIDLE WAY

Rectory Manor Centre of the Croydon Boys' Club were "first in the field" when their leader, Mr. R. P. Down, and Ronald Brooker, the leading member of the club's horse riding section, led the first organised group of riders over the newly opened 80-mile "Ridgeway Bridle Route" from Alfriston, Eastbourne, to Buriton, near Petersfield, Hampshire.

Riding over 20 miles a day and camping at prearranged camp sites along the route, the group arrived at the end of the journey on time, despite having to leave one pony behind because of lameness and finding that the Sussex flints over the Downs made progress much slower than anticipated.

The purpose of the trek was to obtain information for the Pony Club of Great Britain which will assist other youth groups hoping to undertake this ride.

Croydon Advertiser, June 14th 1963

SMALL DOLE
YOUNG RIDERS ON A DOWNLAND TREK

Eight riders, aged 14 to 16 (six girls and two boys) set out on Sunday morning from Mannings Farm, Horton Corner, Small Dole, on an eight-day pony trek along much of the South Downs long-distance bridleway. Those who complete the test by Sunday afternoon should easily qualify for the Duke of Edinburgh's gold award. The riders first went out to the eastern extremity of the route at Birling Gap, and were due back at Small Dole yesterday. They continue on to Littlegreen, near Compton, where they will again turn about, arriving back at Small Dole on Sunday. The riders are from Small Dole, Henfield, Albourne and Shoreham. In charge of the party is Mr. R. P. Down, leader of Henfield Youth Club. They are camping out each night in lightweight tents carried on their mounts. The entire route measures about 170 miles, and travelling more than 20 miles a day, they will tend to their ponies, make and break camp, and cook their own meals.

West Sussex Gazette, 1966

```
        PONY  TREKKING   EXPEDITION EQUIPMENT.
P  sonal.  Sleeping Bag.            Toilet Kit.
          Gilwel Set.              Towel.(Muslin).
          Knife. F.&S. Mug.        Thermos Flask.
          Torch.                   ½Doz Plastic Bags
          Anorak.                  Waterproof.
          Thick Jersy.             Plimsoles.
          Spare Socks.             Spare Underware.
          Spare Jods or Slacks.Hard hat.
          Waterproof covers for Sleeping Bag etc.

   Pony.  Saddle Panniers.         Saddle Blanket.
          Headcollar.              Rope for H.C.
          Grooming Kit.            Tack sponge & soap
          Canvas Bucket.

F  each Pair.
              I. Tent (Complete).
              I. Cooking Stove     Spare fuel.
              I.Set Maps.          Compas.
              I.Notebook.          Pencil.
              I. Trowel.           Toilet paper.
              I.Tin opener.        Matches.
              First Aid Kit.       Emergency Rations.
                   Food for the Day.

F  each  roup.
              Vehicle or Pack Pony and Pack saddle.
              Rations.
              Fodder.
              Tents.
              Spare. Cooking stove.
                     First Aid Kit.
                     Rope.
              Small  ake.  etc. etc.
```

Expedition equipment

RECOMMENDATIONS FOR THOSE PLANNING TO TREK THE RIDGEWAY ROUTE

Careful planning is essential

The going is not all over wide open Downland, many miles of it are now being cultivated right to the top and the going is very flinty. This makes it necessary to keep plenty of time in hand for emergencies and leading ponies etc.

Camp sites

There are very few sites on the whole route where a party could camp on the Ridge, even if permission were obtained. A list of possible helpers, regarding camp sites with grazing, is attached. We hope that this will be enlarged as time goes on.

Would be trekers should contact those they anticipate seeking help from in good time, as it may not always be convenient to use the sites. On no occasion should any of these people be descended on without prior arrangement. Their goodwill is essential for others who may follow.

A good knowledge of lightweight camping is important. Remember to leave your camp site spotless and know your "Country Code", copies of which can be obtained from the National Parks Commission, 1, Cambridge Gate, Regents Park, London, N.W.1., along with a description of the route.

Leadership

It is essential that someone in the party can read a map and compass. Maps 181, 182, 183 Ordinance Survey are needed, nothing less 1" to 1 mile scale will be of any use. An Orienteering compass was found to be ideal for the job and will be needed continuously, unless there is a local guide.

It is essential that an experienced Horseman is IN CHARGE of the party, controlling pace, rests, watering etc., inexperience on this route could cause hardship to ponies.

Unless Trekers are really experienced riders and light weight campers, it would be advisable to:-

a) Have supporting transport and staff to take equipment from site to site and make and strike camp etc.

or

b) Take pack ponies or panniers on each pony and not attempt more than ten miles a day to start with. Remember those hills do not show up on a map! Both panniers and pack equipment need experience in fitting and time for the ponies to get used to them before going on the trek. They must be carefully packed and balanced with no projections on the inside where it can rub the pony and the weight calculated in relation to the rider's weight and pony's ability.

Ponies

All ponies must be fit, used to climbing hills and used to the weight and equipment they will have to carry. They should be used to being turned out together before going away. A "Bully" can keep a tired pony on the move for hours when it ought to be resting. They should be easy to catch.

Shoes

All ponies need shoeing within a few days of going on this trip, if you want to get through without trouble. Ponies with a tendency to "Thin Sole" should have leather under their shoes for protection against the flints. It might help them all!

Water

Water is scarce but if every opportunity is taken, sufficient. BEWARE of water troughs that are contaminated by Weed Killer spray. Nearly all those not on Pastureland were so at the beginning of June.

Planning the Ridgeway Route

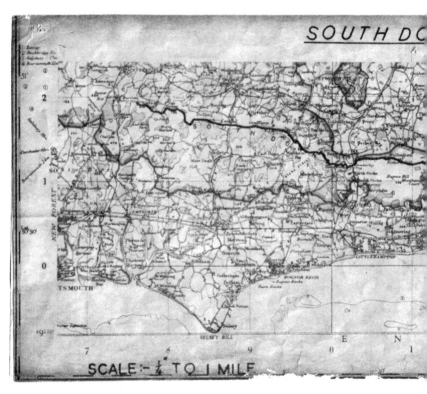

Southdowns Bridleway

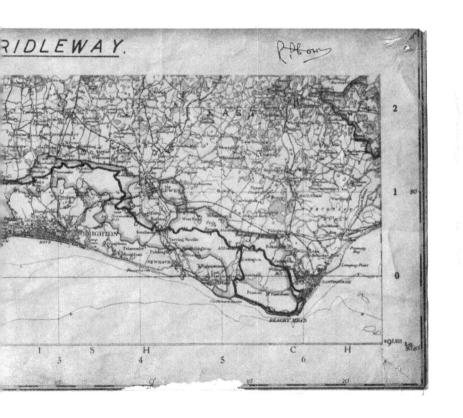

TEENAGE RIDERS ARE TREKKING 80 MILES

THE most ambitious and exacting pony trek yet tackled under the West Sussex County Council-sponsored mounted expeditions starts from Mannings Farm, Small Dole, on Sunday morning.

Eight teenage riders, nearly all of them from the Henfield area, under trek leader Paul Down, Henfield, will ride the 80-mile Downlands bridleway twice over in eight days, camping out each night in lightweight tents.

Small Dole being situated about halfway along the length of the winding long-distance bridleway, the riders, the youngest 15 and all but two of them girls, will head east on Sunday

Averaging 20 miles a day, working in pairs, they will cook for themselves, tend their ponies, which will be put out to grass each night, read maps, put first-aid knowledge to good use if needed, and practice with common-sense what they have been learning during many weeks of intensive training.

By Wednesday they should be back for an overnight stop at Small Dole, having in the meantime ridden out to the eastern limit of the bridleway near Eastbourne and back again.

Inspection

On Wednesday evening or Thursday morning they and their mounts will be inspected by Major Bowden, visiting commissioner of the Pony Club and a member of the Pony Club expeditions' committee.

If they pass the inspection they go on. If they fail, if a pony is found unfit to continue, they will retire, leaving the others to tackle the second leg of the long double journey.

The second stage of the three counties trek will take them by Amberley to Littlegreen near Compton in Hampshire. They will bed down in the Amberley area on Thursday and Saturday next week arriving back at Small Dole ground lunchtime on August 7.

In addition to continuous riding experience all of the young riders have been practising lightweight camping. It was laid down in the beginning that only riders of about Pony Club "B" standard would be allowed to take part.

Paul Down, the trek leader, said in Henfield this week: "They are a keen bunch. If they come through this test they will have completed what probably have been the tou ride ever done in this part o country."

Printed in Great Britain
by Amazon